DOLPHINS

COMMON DOLPHINS

JOHN F. PREVOST
ABDO & Daughters

Published by Abdo & Daughters, 4940 Viking Drive, Suite 622, Edina, Minnesota 55435.

Library bound edition distributed by Rockbottom Books, Pentagon Tower, P.O. Box 36036, Minneapolis, Minnesota 55435.

Printed in the United States.

Cover Photo credit: Peter Arnold, Inc.
Interior Photo credits: Peter Arnold, Inc.

Edited by Bob Italia

Library of Congress Cataloging-in-Publication Data

Prevost, John F.
        Common dolphins / by John F. Prevost.
            p. cm. — (Dolphins)
    Includes bibliographical references (p. 23) and index.
    ISBN 1-56239-496-7
    1. Common dolphin—Juvenile literature. [1. Common dolphin. 2. Dolphins.]
    I. Title. II. Series: Prevost, John F. Dolphins.
    QL737.C432P742   1995
    599.5'3—dc20
                                                                95-12363
                                                                    CIP
                                                                    AC

ABOUT THE AUTHOR

John Prevost is a marine biologist and diver who has been active in conservation and education issues for the past 18 years. Currently he is living inland and remains actively involved in freshwater and marine husbandry, conservation and education projects.

Contents

COMMON DOLPHINS AND FAMILY

Common dolphins live in the world's warm-**temperate** and **tropical** oceans. Dolphins are small-toothed whales. Whales are **mammals**. Like humans, they breathe air with lungs, are **warm blooded**, and feed their young milk.

Common dolphins are one of the most widespread and numerous dolphins. They are also known as the saddleback, cape, and Pacific dolphin. The common dolphin's relatives are the spotted, spinner and striped dolphins.

Common dolphins are one of the most widespread and numerous dophins.

SIZE, SHAPE AND COLOR

Common dolphins differ in size and color. They are 5.5 to 8 feet (1.7 to 2.5 meters) long. Males are slightly larger than females.

Common dolphins have slender, streamlined bodies and long, tapered **flippers**. Most are black on the upper back, white on the underside, and tan or cream colored on their sides. They may have a saddle or hourglass pattern along their sides where the three different colored areas touch.

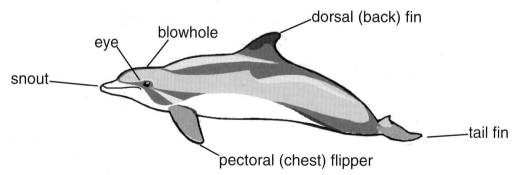

Most dolphins share the same features.

Common dolphins have slender, streamlined bodies that make them excellent swimmers.

Fins and **snout** may be black, white or striped. Stripes may run down the sides or connect the **flippers** to the snout. Some common dolphins may have a black patch around their eyes.

WHERE THEY LIVE

Common dolphins are found worldwide in **temperate** and **tropical** seas. Most groups live near the surface far offshore. Other groups are found in **coastal** areas or in smaller seas. The Mediterranean, Black Sea, and Persian Gulf each have their own groups.

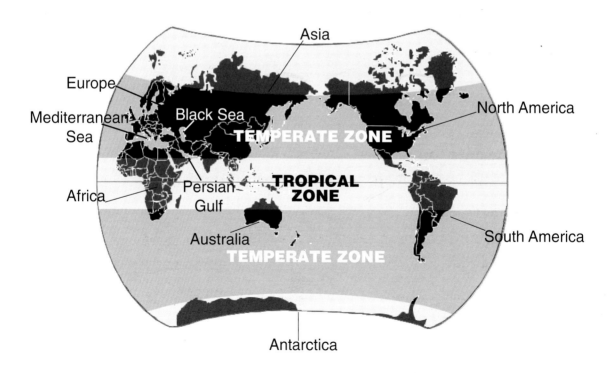

These dolphins are swimming near a ship's bow.

Common dolphins can dive as deep as 918 feet (280 meters). They are often seen riding the **bow waves** of ships and large whales.

Common dolphins travel with other dolphins and whales. Pacific groups also travel with yellowfin tuna. They live in large **pods** of over 100 members. **Migrating herds** may number over 1,000.

SENSES

Common dolphins and people have 4 of the same senses. Their eyesight is good and they can see well in or out of the water. Common dolphins are excellent jumpers and will often leap above the water to look around.

Hearing is their most important sense. Toothed whales have their own **echolocation**. By making a series of clicks and whistles, these dolphins can "see" underwater by listening to the returning echoes.

HOW ECHOLOCATION WORKS

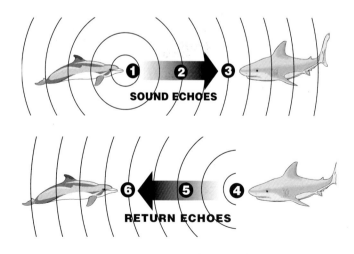

SOUND ECHOES

RETURN ECHOES

The dolphin sends out sound echoes (1). These echoes travel in all directions through the water (2). The sound echoes reach an object in the dolphin's path (3), then bounce off it (4). The return echoes travel through the water (5) and reach the dolphin (6). These echoes let the dolphin know where the object is, how large it is, and how fast it is moving.

Dolphins are excellent jumpers and will often leap high above the water surface.

Common dolphins are **social** animals that touch each other to **communicate**. These dolphins have a sense of taste, but lack the sense of smell.

DEFENSE

Large sharks and killer whales feed on common dolphins. The dolphins' well-developed sense of hearing allows the **pods** to listen for danger and **communicate** warnings. Their best defense is speed and quickness. Young dolphins and weak adults are the most likely **prey**.

Unlike many other dolphin **species**, common dolphins have few problems with tuna nets which often trap and kill dolphins. Common dolphins can escape the nets easier than the spinner and spotted dolphins. Scientists do not know why.

Common dolphins travel in pods and communicate by using echolocation.

FOOD

Common dolphins feed on **schooling** fish and **squid** in deep water. They use their **echolocation** to find **prey** in dark water where they cannot see.

Common dolphins have 40 to 58 pairs of short, sharp teeth per jaw. Their teeth are made to grab prey, not to cut or chew.

Common dolphins **migrate**. The **pods** follow the migration paths of their prey. Pod members **communicate** with each other to hunt **herring**, **sardines**, **smelt** and other small schooling fish.

Common dolphins work in large schools to gather food. These dolphins are in the Sea of Cortez, Baja Mexico.

BABIES

A baby common dolphin is called a **calf**. At birth, a calf is 30 to 35 inches (76 to 89 centimeters) long. Like other **mammals**, the mother makes milk for her calf. Other females in the **pod** will help "baby-sit" the calf while the mother is feeding. These females are related to the mother either as sisters or **offspring**.

In some pods, females with calves may form their own group. Calves will **nurse** for over a year. The young dolphins will not become adults until they are 3 to 7 years old.

A pod of female dolphins protect the calves.

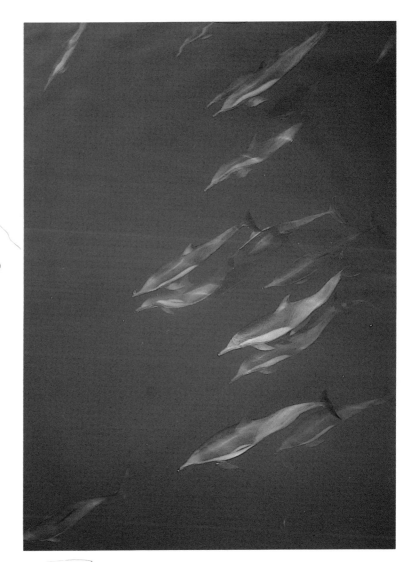

COMMON DOLPHIN FACTS

Scientific Name: *Delphinus delphis*
Synonyms, or scientific names of regional species
    now considered as *D. delphis:*
    D. capensis, D. bairdi, D. tropicalis,
    and *D. delphis ponticius.*

Average Size: 5.5 to 8 feet (1.7 to 2.5 meters).
        Males are often larger than females.

Where They're found: Warm-**temperate** and
        tropical waters of the
        Atlantic, Pacific, and Indian
        oceans as well as the
        smaller seas.

Common dolphins.

GLOSSARY

BOW WAVES - Water pushed up by the front of a ship.

CALF - A baby dolphin.

COASTAL (KOE-stull) - Bordering on water, shore.

COMMUNICATE (kuh-MEW-nih-kate) - To show feelings.

ECHOLOCATION (ek-oh-low-KAY-shun) - The use of sound waves to find objects underwater.

FLIPPERS - The forelimbs of a sea mammal.

HERD - A group of animals of one kind.

HERRING (HAIR-ing) - A small food fish of the North Atlantic Ocean.

MAMMAL - A group of warm-blooded animals that feed their young with the milk from the mother's breast.

MIGRATE - To move from one place to another with the changing seasons.

NURSE - To feed a child or young animal from its mother's breasts.

OFFSPRING - The young of an animal.

POD - A herd or school of sea mammals.

PREY - Animals that are eaten by other animals.

SARDINES - One of several kinds of small fish preserved in oil for food.

SCHOOL - A large number of the same kind of fish or water animals swimming together.

SMELT - A small food fish with silvery scales.

SNOUT - The part of an animal's head that extends forward and contains the nose, mouth, and jaws.

SOCIAL - Living or liking to live with others.

SPECIES - A group of related living things that have common traits.

SQUID - Sea animals related to the octopus that are streamlined in shape and have at least ten arms.

TEMPERATE (TEM-prit) - Moderate to cool water located between the polar and tropical waters.

TROPICAL (TRAH-pih-kull) - The part of the Earth near the equator where the oceans are very warm.

WARM-BLOODED - An animal whose body temperature remains the same and warmer than the outside air or water temperature.

Index

BIBLIOGRAPHY

Cousteau, Jacques-Yves. *The Whale, Mighty Monarch of the Sea.* N.Y.: Doubleday, 1972.

Dozier, Thomas A. *Whales and other Sea Mammals.* Time-Life Films, 1977.

Leatherwood, Stephen. *The Sierra Club Handbook of Whales and Dolphins.* San Francisco, California: Sierra Club Books, 1983.

Minasian, Stanley M. *The World's Whales.* Washington, D.C.: Smithsonian Books, 1984.

Ridgway, Sam H., ed. *Mammals of the Sea.* Springfield, Illinois: Charles C. Thomas Publisher, 1972.